CALIFORNIA
COVERED BRIDGES
PRE 1900'S

Forrest Oldham

To order additional copies of this book, contact:
Xlibris
1-888-795-4274
www.Xlibris.com
Orders@Xlibris.com

CONTENTS

PREFACE

I believe books are a semi-permanent look into the author's history of experiences and relationships to others that all come together to share, with those interested, their collective wisdom and/or facts to that point in time. This is true for me. A number of years ago I joined a photo club to keep me immersed with others that shared the same interest, not only for me to help others, as permitted, but for me to learn more about photography and also get ideas for other life's experiences as the photography brought me there. I was fortunate as a youngster to be given a Brownie Camera and to have enough allowance to afford film to push through that little box. I pulled the shutter on many, many subjects, vacations, holidays and some things many would not think to turn the lens to. One such was photos of the various items I put under my microscope, another gift to my inquisitive mind. I had to carefully focus the microscope then just as carefully hold still the camera over the eyepiece of the microscope, so as not to knock the thing out of focus, then push the shutter without shaking too much. I made many such photos, some of which I retain, thanks to my Mom's safe keeping over the years. Subsequently I graduated to an SLR camera with a couple lenses. Many trips to the library to read up on famous photographers' advice on how to take better and more varied photos led to challenging myself to make, versus take, different types of photos, such as low light, night time, and others. Thank you Ansel Adams, Galen Rowell, and a host of others. I was often frustrated with having to wait for the film development to find if I were successful.

Advance to the digital age and instant gratification in seeing the photos nearly immediately. This began to really improve my skills, my ability to know more quickly how to approach a subject and so on. I also kept hearing "Self Assign". I assigned myself the tasks of learning each of the camera's controls and functions with the resulting images. This was when I joined the photo club. The club President one time asked me if I would lead the monthly photo excursions to various places with various subjects to be had. Earlier experiences with me in another club, a fly fishing club, taught me that the real learner in a teaching environment was the teacher as you had to know your subject well to share it or you were most likely going to be embarrassed with your lack of said knowledge! Knowing this I accepted the challenge. I wanted to take up a notch the event and led the first excursion to "The End of the World". This is a mountain top in the California Gold Country named by a miner during the Gold Rush. Not really photogenic, but it put us out in the field where there were other items, in this case a little known redwood forest. The next month I announced our trip to "Timbucktoo", not the one in Africa, the one north of Sacramento and east of Marysville. Again, not photogenic, a plaque noting the site of a Gold Rush Town with that name. I had another destination in mind with a backup to that. This was, as it turns out, though I did not know at the time, the longest free span Covered Bridge in the world, depending on how you measure and define the measure of such. It was well received by the group on our trip. For a topping to this we proceeded to another not well known covered bridge, again well received followed by a trip to a large gold mining site now a state park!

Shortly after these excursions, with my curiosity in high gear, and some research on the computer, I found there were close to 100 covered bridges of one sort or another in California and decided to self-assign the task of photographing as many of them as I could. Other events in my life afforded the opportunity to travel the state, and over time, accomplish this task.

I then asked myself, "What do I do with all this?. I pondered this over a few years. During this time I joined another photo group and through participating with them discovered a computer program that would make slide shows with a large variety of transitions, titles, music and other features that when combined could make interesting viewing. I bought the program, learned it using it for a couple of simple programs and set about putting my photos together about the Covered Bridges into some shows in which I divided them into three groups, The Pre-1900 Historical, Privately Built, and those cities and states would build and maintain. This I followed with the question, "I wonder how many books there are about Covered Bridges in California?" I was unable to find even one, at the time, now I know of one from quite some time ago which I purchased as a used copy..

Not only was I to find out about much of this through research on the computer, I would also talk about my projects to those I encountered and friends. One such friend insisted there was a covered bridge in Coloma, the original California Gold Rush site which he claimed to have seen on one of his 1920's Dodge Car Club Drives. I stated to him I had an "official list" of the Covered Bridges of California registered with the State of California and it was not on the list! He persisted. A couple days later, I grabbed my camera, invited my obliging wife, filled the tank and went to see for myself if such bridge existed. It did not. We found a few other things to photograph on the trip and began asking around about the bridge. After many, many encounters with several of the State Park Rangers a light bulb went on with one that was overhearing the conversation and volunteered she thought there was a picture of one in one of their smaller publications they use for fund raising. We found the photo and it is believed to be the very first covered bridge in the Western United States! It was by a photographer that is supposed to be the very first to photograph Yosemite, also! More research and I was able to buy the rights to that old black and white photo. This led to even more research on the history of these bridges, some of which I put into the slide shows and this book. There is also a plethora of engineering information to be had about the construction of these bridges which I do not get into too deeply.

Now comes the good part for me. Thank you, Betti Clark for asking me to lead the photo trips, the other club members for their participation and encouragement, Gold Rush Chapter of Photographers Society of America, for opening my eyes to fine photography and it's presentation, Richard "Buzz" Horn for putting me on the first Covered Bridge, my wife, Maria for putting up with me and encouraging me on this and many other projects, my Mom for providing materials to satisfy my curiosities early on, photographic authors for much know how and inspiration, and many, many others too numerous to mention!

What follows is intended as an introduction with photos to the remaining structures built before 1900 and not intended to be a definitive work on the subject.

INTRODUCTION

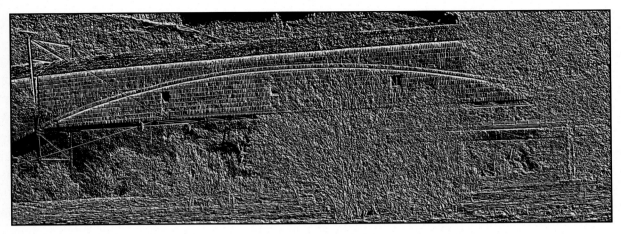

Nye's Crossing Covered Bridge with a little darkroom editing

Living in California I feel fortunate to have stumbled upon the covered bridges of California and their history. Furthermore, I feel a responsibility to share what I have learned at least a little bit, enough to maybe pique the curiosity of those that pick up this work to the degree they will further read and research about the subject as it relates to their interests or perhaps a project of their own. This book is not intended by me to be the last answer on the subject of California's covered bridge history, just a peek at a small part of it with more publications to come on other covered bridges visualized and constructed later in California's march to one of the nation's, if not the world's, powerhouse economies. The permission to build these structures was one of the first acts of the newly formed California government's legislature for the benefit of the economy relative to the 1849 Gold Rush. The bridges and many other entrepreneurial enterprises of the era were arguably important contributors to the Gold Rush where many only have heard of the gold and the mining of the gold as the important historical event. This economic process played out in many, many other places in the west with many, many other natural resources being harvested such as timber, silver, copper, and uranium ore. Each of these resources needed to be moved to where they could be processed and distributed to their end users, often carried over one or more of these covered bridges. Many bridge builders and operators did well financially with their investments in these structures. Even today the remains of many of these operations, though not operating, keep a small portion of California's economy going as people such as myself and some of my friends visit the historical sites to learn of them and photograph them. This process has us buying gas, meals, entrance fees, and other such that keeps money moving through our western states. A couple of these older bridges also host other functions that bring benefits to their communities, such as Civil War Reenactments. These events are anticipated strongly and attended by many each year! Other experiences can be easily combined with an expedition to many of these bridges. I will share some of this extra knowledge with you, the reader, as I lay out a little bit of the information I have accumulated about these wonderful structures. It is my hope you are able to glean a little from this offering to help you discover something of interest to you in your journey of life. Thank you for taking the time to view my work.

BIRTH OF CALIFORNIA

The story of the Covered Bridges of California begins with the beginning of California which, in turn, is the result of politics and the need for natural resources. John Sutter established what we know as Sutter's Fort in Sacramento as well as other industries nearby such as his Hock Farm near, now, Yuba City. Another project, supervised by James Wilson Marshall, was being built on the American River east of Sacramento in the foothills, to provide lumber needed to support the other industries' structure needs. In 1848 Marshall was walking a water raceway used to divert water to the mill and observed a shiny spot among the gravel. This was shared quietly with John Sutter and found to be a rather significant piece of gold. The pair agreed to go about harvesting this mineral without informing others, however, word was spread somehow gold was in the hills of California and thus started the California Gold Rush of 1849. At the same time the United States was at war with Mexico which settled by 1850 with California becoming the 31st state.

Late in 1849 through early 1850 California's leaders created the California Constitution in which the first acts were to establish various rights to it's resources. One such was the right and registration of mine site ownership. The legislators also used the Eastern United States Riparian Water Rights Model to lay out water possessions. One such was a person that lives next to a waterway has right to use that water, later to be modified to include what is known as "Appropriative Right" in which a person or entity could have "Legal Physical Control" of a water source not immediately related to their nearby property ownership based on "beneficial public use" allowing for the buying, selling, and trade of water. Today Article X, Section 2 of the State Constitution states that "All water use be reasonable and beneficial." This is legalize to say "Let's fight this out in court." This becomes very important in years to follow as water was used for many reasons in the process of mining the gold and all the supportive industries.

Another act of the Constitutional Leaders was to permit private parties to build bridges over waterways and charge a toll for those using it. Again the Eastern States model of transport economics was employed. They used a "Turnpike" system between 1792 and 1845 and began using a "Plank Road" in 1847 until 1853. I leave it to the reader to research what each of these is. Often town governments managed the roads sometimes to the displeasure of the citizens. It was also found that people would circumvent toll collections on the land roads, however, this was much more difficult for water crossings. In 1850 the California State Legislature passed the "General Laws of Incorporation." which allowed business alliances. In addition, thinking came to the conclusion that private enterprise did a better job of managing roads and bridges than government due to the profit motive. In 1853 additional laws gave authority to the counties to manage these transportation facilities as they saw fit, many of which were happy to let the private entities manage them and just assess taxes for the privilege. It was also widely known that for an economy to thrive resources needed to move about efficiently. Collectively, all this led to the construction of over 100 toll bridges in the Gold Country, many being covered bridges.. Incidentally, much of this same activity spilled over into Oregon at the same time, with many covered bridges from this time still standing.

THE GOLD RUSH

Auburn greets visitors with history and cheer as two look for gold

Many present day towns and cities claim to be the gateways to the Gold Rush, the two biggest being Auburn and Placerville, the latter nicknamed "Hangtown". These are at the northern and southern ends of California Highway 49, otherwise known as the Gold Rush Highway, with Coloma, the real center of the event, roughly equidistant between them. Each is rich in Gold Rush History and well worth a trip for those interested. There are many lesser towns with interesting histories throughout the area and beyond, with some that were bigger than either of these in their heyday. Their demise was due to other choices made, such as where to place freeways and highways, or reduction in the amount of ore, perhaps difficulty in retrieving it. The earliest seeking of gold was around Coloma following the secret getting out that James Marshall found gold at Sutter's Mill. A number of bridges of various sorts sprung up on the American River nearby, one of which was a lengthy covered bridge, now lost to history, except for a rare photo by an early photographer named Charles Leander Weed. Weed was also fortunate, or determined enough to be recognized currently as the first to photograph in Yosemite! He owned a photo studio on what is now J St. in Sacramento. The bridge is considered, with latest information at hand, to be the earliest covered bridge constructed in the west, though some believe another obscure bridge further away may be first for the covered variety.

Early on more simple bridges, one constructed by Jim Stephens in 1849, a foot bridge, with a toll of 25 cents per crossing. Another, a year later, big enough for wagons, built by John Little and Edward Raun, collected $20 in tolls in 3 months. This was good money for the times! Little was a big player in the bridge building business of the time with his skills coming from his experience in building East

Coast bridges. The Coloma Covered Bridge, constructed in 1852 by Little, was based on the East Coast covered bridge construction. It lasted at least until 1858 when Weed made the photo shared here with permission from the County of El Dorado Historic Museum. A newer iron constructed bridge takes it's place a short distance away with a small sign explaining the difficulties of bridge building in the region.

These bridges were often not large load worthy like modern bridges and one collapsed from the weight of a herd of cattle. Signs posted to instruct users of the rules of passage limited the number of wagons and animals on the bridge at one time and were often misspelled such as "NOTIS!" for "NOTICE!" which reflected the lack of education at the time.

Coloma Covered Bridge, built 1852,, the earliest known photo of the first Covered Bridge in the West by Charles L. Weed 1858 courtesy of the El Dorado Historic Museum of Placerville, CA

Close up of the bridge in the top photo

Though grainy, one can see the similarity to the construction of the Wawona Covered Bridge in this magnified portion of the original photo by Weed. The exterior bracing helped the structure of the bridge

WHY MAKE A COVERED BRIDGE?

Many, including myself initially, believe the bridges were covered to prevent snow and other weather related reasons to keep the bridges safe and not slippery. Many are familiar with these beautiful bridges of the Eastern United States where snow is often encountered. This, however, is not the reason, though a benefit, of the coverings. The structural members of the bridge are the most necessary, expensive, and hardest to repair with the coverings being only a sacrificial, easily, and inexpensively replaced item to contribute to the longevity of the structures. The coverings often were more practical than pleasing, though, most are nice to the eyes. Many different coverings were used, mostly based on the local materials at hand, which was also true of the structural members, some of which were harvested from some distance away. The practicality of these decisions remain with us today as a good many of these structures still stand.

At the time of this photo, around 2010, the bridge was considered unsafe for other than foot traffic. The structural members were still in relatively good shape with the weathered covering falling off in places.

WOODEN TRUSS DESIGNS

KINGPOST

QUEENPOST

BURR ARCH

WARREN

HOWE

PRATT

STEEL THREADED RODS
TENSION MEMBERS

WOODEN HEAVY MEMBERS
VERTICAL SUPPORTS

VERY LARGE WOODEN BEAMS
HORIZONTAL PIECES

Drawings are representative
only and not to scale.

Most relatively short span bridges used one of the top two styles of trusses.
As longer spans were needed the lower three types of trusses were employed.
Extreme spans required extreme designs such as the Burr Arch.
One of the longest lasting and longest spans, The Bridgeport Covered Bridge,
constructed of very large timbers, is a composite of the Burr Arch, Howe, and
Pratt Trusses.

STRUCTURAL TYPES

Most covered bridges are set upon concrete abutments and columns with the wooden members assembled in various ways for the structural spanning between. The covering is then applied over additional supporting members depending on the choice of material. Following is a list of some of the structural types, each with a beauty of it's own.

Stringer– Simplest, being only large timbers set across short spans with the remaining structure built on top. Often some of the cross pieces were left long to create braces seen from the outside of the bridge.

Kingpost-Adding a strong vertical timber to the center of longer stringers with diagonal timbers attached to the apex and ends allowed for longer spans than simple stringer.

Queenpost-To allow for even longer spans, two vertical members, called Queenposts, were placed roughly each one third the way in from the ends with diagonals between the tops and the ends of the stringers. Another short "stringer" was placed between the tops of the Queenposts.

Warren Truss-Basically a series of alternating diagonal members attached to the stringers with a stringer attached to the tops of each. This allowed for slightly longer spans, yet.

Howe Truss-Uses opposing diagonals from each end supporting a top stringer (chord) with the addition of threaded steel rods, washers, and nuts vertically for tension. The nuts can be tightened as time goes by to take out sagging of the truss.

Pratt-Turned upside down the Howe Truss concept using vertical wooden members to support the upper stringer (chord) with the threaded rods installed diagonally between the verticals and the upper/ lower stringers (chords).

Smith Truss-Crossing members were sandwiched together to support top and bottom chords with threaded steel rods installed intermeshing these to provide compressive and tension strength of the structure.

Sometimes combinations of these and other structural concepts were combined for even greater spans. One such very successful one is the Burr Arch, another being Pratt &King.

For additional reading on this subject, I suggest "Covered Bridges of the West" by Kramer A Adams as well as other research on bridge engineering.

More will be shared about this as we investigate the remaining pre 1900 covered bridges individually in the pages to follow.

AKA-BACKWARDS COVERED BRIDGE
AKA-FREEMAN'S CROSSING

Built in 1860 in the Queen Truss structure, the Oregon Creek Covered Bridge is the oldest remaining in California at this writing, with many years to go as you will find with further reading of this offering. It is called the "Backwards Covered Bridge" due to it's being reset on it's footings by pulling it back onto them with log rollers and an oxen team following it's washing away as a complete unit by the breaking of the English Dam in 1883 due to flood waters. When first I visited, it was covered in vertical planks and metal corrugated roofing to protect the structure, much of which is in disrepair. Due to it's condition, only foot traffic is allowed to cross.

This bridge is found north of the town of North San Juan on highway 49. A fast falling driveway to a "Day Use Park" is the only sign for the pull off to the right of the highway. Many locals use the park for fishing and a nearby swimming hole. One must want to find this one to experience it!

One of the cultural aspects of the covered bridges was their use for local notices, art work and such, that today we call "Graffiti", which you can see here. Notice, too, the large beams in the lower sides of the structure that are the "Queen Truss" system.

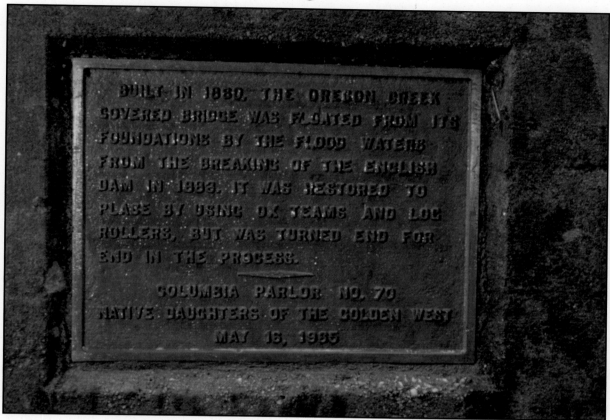

There are a number of organizations that look after historical artifacts as this. Often they leave in place durable plaques detailing the history and the caretakers. In this case the Daughters of the Golden West take up the responsibility. These organizations will hold fund raising events to collect money for the upkeep which we are fortunate to have that we can experience them for ourselves. Like other groups that work on our behalf I would like to thank these people for their efforts.

NYES CROSSING COVERED BRIDGE

AKA-BRIDGEPORT COVERED BRIDGE
AKA-WOOD'S CROSSING

Spanning one of the clearest waters, built in 1862 over the South Yuba River, Nyes Crossing Covered Bridge shares the distinction with an Eastern United States covered bridge as being the longest free span covered bridge in the world, depending upon how measured. It is currently the second oldest remaining covered bridge in California and is a State Park. Funding has been secured to refurbish and preserve the structure for pedestrian use. This was the first covered bridge I visited in California with my photography club. Though recognized by a number of organizations for it's historical importance, which the most notable is the National Register of Historic Places #71000168. It was constructed to meet the transportation needs of the Nevada (County) Comstock Lode.

David Isaac John Wood saw a need for a crossing of the mighty Yuba River and using lumber from his mill in Sierra County built a Composite Howe/Burr Arch structured bridge as part of the Virginia Turnpike Company Toll Road. The California legislature permitted such as one of it's first acts. At 233 feet, it is a spectacle to appreciate, having no supports in the middle and constructed only of wooden components and a few steel rods. Much of the wooden elements are themselves massive.

A look at the underside of Nye's Crossing shows the bottom of the wooden
pieces and the vertical steel rods used to construct the bridge.

STRUCTURAL DETAILS

Looking out one of the windows gives a sense of scale of the structural pieces as well as the richness of color of the wood that remains due to the protection from the weathering elements. Graffiti can also be observed on many wooden members, some from long ago.

The weather has taken a toll on the exterior coverings which have held surprisingly well. Also observed is the modern day assistance of steel and cabling to ensure integrity of the bridge until the refurbishing work is completed. The shingles, being easily and inexpensively replaced when compared to the structural elements, help to guarantee long life of the water crossing.

STRUCTURAL DETAILS

Looking down the length of the inside of John Wood's efforts can be seen the arch truss as well as the Howe inspired vertical and cross pieced members that have served so well for a great many years. This photo makes the bridge look short. Remember the scale of the wooden beams is massive!

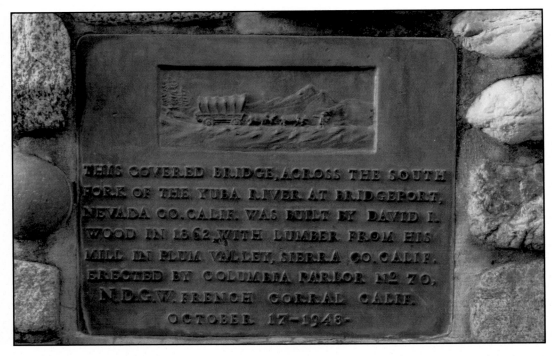

Nye's Crossing Covered Bridge has been recognized many times over the years for it's accomplishments. In 1948 the Columbia Parlor No. 70 N.D.G.W. of French Corral, CA was the first followed in 1964 by the California State Park Commission partnering with both the Nevada County Historical Society and Chapter No. 10 E. Clampus Vitus. Wm. B Meek/Wm. M Stewart are/were significant members in these efforts.

Wood's Crossing is currently undergoing restoration for use as a pedestrian bridge to add to a hiking path established a number of years ago along the Yuba River. It is among one of the first to help enable some handicapped individuals enjoy the historical sites and outdoors of California.

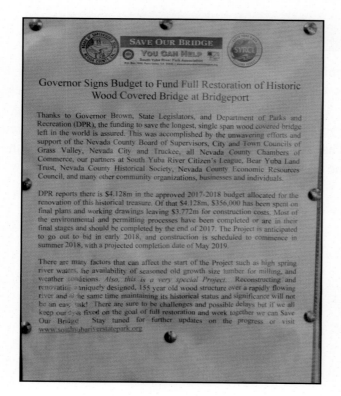

A large group of organizations shared the responsibility of making sure the funding is available to maintain and restore this valuable historical part of California's and the United States' history as made notice in this posting on the bridge.

The covered bridges were built to enable convenient travel and transportation to support the efforts of the California Gold Rush. Along many of the routes were other towns and structures to support the process as well. Of course, Wells Fargo was a part of this. This building can be found north of Nye's Crossing a short way and short while past this you can treat yourself to the newly restored Oregon Creek Covered Bridge AKA– The Backwards Covered Bridge. The towns of Grass Valley and Nevada City are in the neighborhood, also. Nearby, the Empire Mine is one of the bigger historical draws of the curious.

The Victorian Past is celebrated in December on the streets of Old Towns Nevada City and Grass Valley. Many people dress the period and enjoy engaging the visitors in the history and joy of that time of year.

NYES CROSSING ALSO KNOWN AS

BRIDGEPORT COVERED BRIDGE

Viewed from the eastern, not so pretty side, measuring 330 feet long with four spans, the Knights Ferry Covered Bridge is considered to be the longest in the United States west of the Mississippi. Located in Stanislaus County, constructed in the Howe Truss style in 1864, this bridge is a local landmark and the center of many events. An earlier open roof truss bridge built in 1857 washed away in a flood was replaced by this durable structure. This local icon is little known by passers-by on the local highway as the signs only refer to a park with historical interests. Gold Rush stakeholders used the original well-traveled road, serviced by this bridge, known as the Stockton Sonora Road, to get to the Gold Country and back.

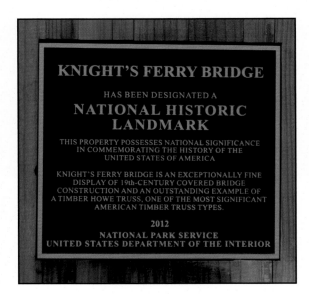

A Plaque states the bridge's status.

One of many events held near this attraction.

Aesthetically pleasing to the eye, late 1800's foundations
were often river rock masonry type structures...

KNIGHT'S FERRY

COVERED BRIDGE

POWDER WORKS COVERED BRIDGE

AKA PARADISE PARK COVERED BRIDGE

Santa Cruz County is thought to currently have the most covered bridges with the originally known as Powder Works Covered Bridge being the flagship bridge. Renamed Paradise Park Covered Bridge by its current Masonic owners, it was built over the San Lorenzo River in 1872. Using the Smith Truss system over two spans it connects the banks of the river 180 feet apart. The Civil War brought a need for a gunpowder factory in the west which was filled by the Powder Works Company in 1861. It supplied explosives for the Gold Rush Miner's needs and the bridge supported the transportation needs of this business. It is currently still in use by vehicles less than 5 tons. There are many points of historical interest nearby and Civil War Re-enactments are held nearby at the Felton Covered Bridge.

The Smith Truss system shown in this photo has proven to be very durable.

The Mason's work very hard to have a positive
impact on the world which is reflected here.

Constructed, depending on historical source, in 1858 or 1868 over the South Fork Merced River, Mariposa County, as an open truss bridge, the Wawona Covered Bridge served as the access point for Yosemite. It primarily allowed hay transporters to move their product to market. A decision to cover it resulted in it becoming a covered bridge in 1875 probably completed in 1875 which is the accepted "build date". Wawona is the only covered bridge in a National Park as far as my research can find. It's horizontal structural members made of Ponderosa Pine, similarly used in other bridges of the time, proved a good choice. Due to the uncovered era and flood damage, the structure showing signs of decay led to a decision to roll the structure to dry land in 1955 to repair it. New exact replacement members hewn with original period type tools were used. It's vertical members were made of Douglas Fir. It was then rolled back in place over the river and is used as a walk bridge currently. I affectionately call it "The Most Seen and Forgotten Covered Bridge" due to many seeing it when arriving at Yosemite's southern entrance and quickly forgetting it when confronted with all of the Park's other sights. Charles Leander Weed, believed to be the first to photograph Yosemite, likely crossed this bridge in it's uncovered state. Photography, in it's infancy at the time, was the daguerreotype, and many such photos survive today to create high quality prints. His first subject was Yosemite Falls.

Located in Yosemite National Park the Wawona Covered Bridge shares the stage with a great number of other fantastic sights, here Bridal Veil Falls with it's predictable rainbow. Yosemite is one of the most visited parks in the National system with large numbers of international travelers arriving yearly.

HONEY RUN COVERED BRIDGE

Built over Butte Creek, Butte County in 1890, Honey Run being not only one of the longer covered bridges, also has the distinction of having a raised roof section in it's middle area. It combines structural styles of Pratt and King trussing to achieve the span. It is said the name comes from a couple of lovers walking nearby that encountered angry bees. "Run! Honey! Run!" was the response by one of the two as they ran across the bridge to make good their escape! Today weddings and other events are held at the bridge that is not too far from the college town of Chico which has other reputations and tourist options. Look up the YOYO Museum! The other direction leads you into the mountains and a town called Paradise, which it seems to be for a good many retirees. It is a gateway to mountain outdoor activities.

The well organized members of the Honey Run structure have worked for quite some time to support the bridge to be used safely even today.

FELTON COVERED BRIDGE

The Felton Covered Bridge is California's youngest, still standing, and built before 1900 covered bridge. As also the tallest in the United States at 35 feet. it became a community project. A pancake breakfast was held yearly to raise funds for restoration and maintenance of the bridge following a citizen protest to it's proposed destruction for a newer alternate material bridge to replace it. The newer bridge was constructed a short distance down the San Lorenzo River thus saving the historical bridge. One of only a few and last constructed of Redwood and using the Pratt Truss for one lone span in 1892, it only entertains foot traffic today. It is located at the rear of a park-in the town of Felton, named for Senator Charles N. Felton. It is the site of Civil War Re-enactments and was listed as California Historical Landmark #583 in July 1969. Santa Cruz County claims to have the most covered bridges in California, Felton being the second oldest after the Powder Works Bridge. Another, The Glen Canyon Covered Bridge over Branciforte Creek, replaced by a modern concrete structure, was one of the most photographed and filmed commercialy.

The author standing inside the Felton Covered Bridge demonstrates it's size.

A Blacksmith's skill shows in hardware of the times.

In July 1969 the Felton Covered Bridge was designated California Historical Landmark #583

THE FUTURE OF THESE BRIDGES

When I first visited this bridge only pedestrians were allowed to pass. We are fortunate that many people today are actively helping to preserve these historical bridges, here the Oregon Creek bridge after it's rehabilitation. Today it is used as a vehicle access to extra parking across the creek for the park.

Due to the extensive time and structural replacements necessary to correct years of wear on possibly the worlds oldest and longest free span covered bridge, outside metal supports are installed. Construction is expected to be completed May 2019. With continued interest in maintaining our history, hopefully other bridges will get similar attention.

Oxbow Ridge Covered Bridge- Fair Oaks, CA

These aesthetically pleasing structures, I believe, serve as inspiration for some modern structures needed for practical use and to accent the main project such as an exclusive housing tract, golf course, or business plaza. Many years before I discovered the California Covered Bridges I worked as a carpenter in the Sacramento area. One project was to set forms and pour the concrete for foundation abutments for a bridge to access a high-end housing development. Much later, while researching and searching out the various bridges on the California list I discovered the above bridge, the one I helped get started years earlier! In a sense, I came full circle on this endeavor due to my curiosities. I encourage each of you to chase yours, if not through these bridges, through other avenues. I believe your life will be enriched by such efforts. Best to you and your journey.

Printed in the United States
By Bookmasters